"Socialism is not a form of Government."

The Democratic Socialism Manifesto

An introduction of sorts:

Most of you who picked this up questioned many different things about the cover, but surly you all came back to the overall question. Who is this guy? And is there some credential (piece of paper) that says he knows what he's talking about. No. What did he just say? I said, No. I was born June 25, 1990 in Las Vegas, Nevada, 6:17p.m. for all the Astrologers reading this. I'm just the average Patriot like you. Living in my 30s right alongside you. I could be your neighbor, or the person next to you now. That's it. A guy who graduated the school system at fifteen, best classes being History and English. Then, I threw it all away, to live a "normal" life. Believe me, if there were time machines, I'd be having some serious talks with the younger me. But this book is not about my life, its Historical Philosophy, it is The Democratic Socialism Manifesto. Policies and Philosophies that are in dire need in this country, in order to bring about a better United States of America, and ultimately world.

So hello, it's nice to meet you. I am a Democratic Socialist.

The Future, Millennials, and America.

Technology is taking over. There's no two ways about it. No stopping it, ever. Now you're probably saying "Kyle there's no way you can know that, what proof do you have?". And to make you feel even less secure, you're right. By the time you read this, all "facts", I could ever present you would be outdated at the time of your reading this. This book is being written in 2024 A.D. the people of this time live in the transition of the new millennium and have not fully accepted that automation is upon them, in the moment. Not fully. They are still clinging on to the belief that they can manage it, stop the impending obsoletion of the Human worker in this country. We are the change, the beginning of the end of Human labor. Some like me have accepted the fact, but most still think, that it is at least a century from being fully implemented, it's not, it began even before the warning of Presidential Candidate Andrew Yang. And Millennials are the ones seeing to it.

Be you a Millennial on the Right, Left, or somewhere in between-you are bringing about the change. Especially if you have taken up politics. Now for those of you long past the Millennial era, and those of you who are still none the less saying "Well, I'm not a Millennial this Manifesto isn't for me." You're wrong, this is for all Humans, a system that will flourish all of mankind, while taking none of the Individuals Rights away. Regardless of what planet you live on. This is for beyond all of us. Oh great, now he's bringing Science Fiction. No, I'm not. For this answer let's look at the previous generation, Generation X. I'm sure we've all heard of the man Elon Musk. Because of his investments, at the time of writing this, we will be seeing the first colonies go to Mars before the Century is out. Powered by the hard work and ingenuity of the work force of the time. Millennials and elder Generation Z. History will show a blanket of ignorance foreshadow the very fabric of The United States, beginning in the year 1909. It was the failed attempt at stopping what is to come, at the, what is-to those of you who are after. Now you might be saying "What happened in 1909?" Wardenclyffe tower happened. This event showed the World that utilities, especially electricity, could be free to everyone, for very low costs to Society in the long run. Which if left to flourish, would have begun the Age I have been speaking of now. This inevitable age of Automation. You know, that need to cut costs and gain more feeling, who had continued in the 1940s, as they begun testing the stolen Tesla files. Needing all that steel, coal, labor, the let the best tech and bombs win mentality. Flow money flow. But that leads us here…

The People have spoken, and the word is Capitalism.

Let this be said, the Corporation is not a person, and in such, should not be afforded the same rights as person. But, nonetheless like any developing Entity, we had to grow through the lashings of poor ideas and decisions. The word Capitalism is misconstrued to fit every greedy person's own agenda or idea of what it means to them. From the person's right to work, to the very amount an employer should get to pay their workers. All the while, the very ideas true meaning gets lost in the greed, in the "that's mine, I worked for it." What is this idea, this undeniable, vibrational, thought pattern? Is it not right for the Individual to make something, anything, then sell it for what they want? Unhindered? Yes and no, Greed is never fair. The Human need to have Freedom to be as inventive or sloth like as it wants, is an underlying tone that has plagued existence since its first thinking creature.

Capitalism was meant as a means of eradicating Greed by giving it access to flourish, to quench it, so that the self-love then must turn outward to be fulfilled. Which as a freethinking being, you know the only other outward action, that fulfills the inner consciousness, is giving. The battle was never expected to be won completely, just off set. Numbers of those choosing to take care of each other and help each other flourishing would be so much larger, that the Greed numbers, would eventually be far and few between. The "Give me more, and let me decide if I want to be nice." people. So, the People of the World have spoken. And the word is Capitalism.

You might be saying but Kyle, you say you're a Democratic-Socialist? Isn't Socialism an economic structure? Well, yes and no. Yes, there is an ideology of Socialism that is economy, and most so called "scholars", would say it is. You know the type, these are the same ones who try to say that metaphors are laced in the words of Jesus when He is saying "Truly I say to you..." It was no different in today's Politics and Philosophies, posing political ideologies against each other to control the people, as it very well may still be at the time of reading of this. But Socialism is far more than that and is based off the study of society: as a whole. To find the perfect balance, where the Human can thrive, not just survive. Even the founder of Communism, which should be only recognized as the Authoritarian Socialism it is, acknowledged that even it could not work without Capitalism being a prerequisite.

So is this a contradiction? Or some term that means something it doesn't? Not necessarily…

The need to be Free, meet the Authoritarian us all.

Democracy is never going away. The need of the Individual will forever out way the need of the Many. And what's worse, over the needs of their own blood relatives in many cases. So, what are we to do in an uncontrollable world? Just let it go? See how the cards lie? I feel not, as I'm sure the person reading this, feels not. The need to be Free, meet the Authoritarian in us all. No need to sugar coat it. We have freedom of speech after all, no matter how badly the Fascists and Dictators want it to go away. This is how you begin spotting the snakes in the grass of the Democratic-Socialism movement, they have lost sight of the main goal, having turned to vengeance and hate. Protecting society, even from itself, is a daunting task. Too much of anything ends up corrupting itself, History shows us that. But something must be done-none the less. This Authoritarian for the Good, this Socialist in us, is what Government always was, and always will be meaning to be. Regardless of how much privacy it is trying to encroach on in the Republic/Democratic sense, or to the downright none, in the Communism/Authoritarian sect. There is a quote that comes to mind every time I meditate on this subject of an Active, what you still call, Government:

"Those who would give up privacy for security, deserve neither privacy nor security."

>Thomas Jefferson-2nd President of The United States of America

This quote holds true, it is a timeless statement of the Individual I mentioned previously, and why the Democratic portion of the Democratic-Socialist movement is so important. It emphasizes the tipping point, and with further study of the Human condition so readily available and accessible in my lifetime, I give you just as meaningful response.

"If the needs of the Individual are met to the point of thriving, there will be no need to worry about security, let alone get to the point of talks of taking privacy for it. Envy will be eliminated, for everyone will have access to what they desire within the realm of Morality and Consumerism."

So, the answer was always simple, what we in the very early millennium still called an active Government. One concerned with its own people's wants and needs. In doing so, making it possible to steer the Citizen's needs into being the help of the whole of Human race, without the Citizens feeling a pinch. So they never lose the desire to spread the Utopia, until all are thriving. Allowing the rest of the Universe to be the fields for the Rebellious lambs of the Individual. This kind of , what I use to also call, Government: sets up Defense Systems to protect its Citizens from the lies of those who wish to profit off them, the Individual says, "Well let me do it in a way everyone profits from it, and what I gain let me fight to the death to keep it, and let everyone do the same." Then, looking at the danger to the lives of Citizens from such a request, of what is the very force, or Socialism, that brings Humans together and protects them, recognizes the need of the Individuals, and lets them self-regulate its consumerism, up to a certain lifestyle of carefree satisfaction. While it focuses on the threats trying to steal from Society at large, which include its very Citizenry.

Well this all sounds good, so what does Socialism even mean?

Socialism, let us talk of iterations and definitions.

Socialism, let us talk of iterations and definitions. Many different dictionaries and political scientists would say it has no true definition. Others that it is a form of Government that takes Freedom from the people. They have no true definition and in so doing, leaving the door wide open for the definition I give you now, the one truest to the word:

Socialism: ~ verb: The need, condition, compulsion, feeling and or force of Nature, that causes Consciousness to seek other forms of Consciousness and to form groups. The force that causes Entities to socialize. ~noun: The Law, Judicial, and Military aspects of Society. The branch of Society that conducts studies on how to maintain and help its selected Territory and Citizens thrive, by understanding its collective actions, that have been monitored throughout a recorded history of existence- and enforces the results by means of Lawmaking, Judicial upholding, and in extreme cases Military intervention. The Institution of Civilization.

Socialist: ~noun~ A person who is working for the Socialism of their selected territory, and area they have chosen to reside, or have been born into.

Socialism is not a form of Government. It is a better, and more true word for this created Institution. No person was meant to Govern or be Governed. There are only those Entities among us who are more inclined to study Society, and its needs, then choose to possess the Will to do something about it. Choice is not meant to happen, that's why it is called choice. Any Citizen can choose to become a Socialist. You have the Democratic Socialism styles, which always have and always will include, all forms of Constitutions and Republics, ones that emphasize the Rights of the Individual. To the Authoritarian Socialism, which is every Tyrant's wet dream, giving an Individual complete Control of the location/territory's Socialism. Each iteration studies Society and does what it feels is best, with or without full Democratic consensus, since sometimes, the Individual loves a Good surprise. And on the flip side, too much control, causing rebellion within the Socialism. Making it more friendly to the Individuals within the Citizenry. So let us talk, be it market or non-market, it is all part of our collective Socialism at the end of the day. Now you may be saying "Well Kyle, that sounds like Sociology in some sense?" That's exactly what Socialism is and does, and then, should be turning to fulfill the needs of the people with its findings: so that they are secure feeling, and full of generosity. Leaving them willing to dive deeper into themselves to find out all that they can be. The word Sociology itself should not exist in some sense, nor should the option of it exist in the sphere of careers of the Citizen: as there is already the Socialism doing that. Oh, I'm sorry, Government.

Democratic Socialism is where all those who love Freedom need to be to calling home. One Party has all that has ever been needed for Freedom, anything more is just exposing a lust for Power, and that is for the Authoritarian Socialist, and that Individual is a threat to Freedom. True Freedom doesn't separate itself; it openly debates with itself, coming to the majority Will ruling, even in Republican Socialism. Hence the term Republican not even being necessary, the majority ruling through a Represenitive is still Democracy, because the majority is still ruling. Thus, Democratic

Socialism. Does this mean you're somehow a bad person? That you want to overthrow the very Constitution that will make the thriving, of both responsible Socialism, and the responsible Individual, flourish? Absolutely not!

When is now the best time to change?

It is a question I am sure will stand the test of time. Continuing to haunt those who only talk of wanting change, because it's too hard to let go of their old habits. Now, for the sake of argument, you see the light, and have decided that now is the best time for change in your Political and Worldly outlook. Let me be the first to say, Welcome to the movement of Human Freedom and Longevity. Tell me: How can I convince you to not become Power hungry? Because even in this upcoming Society, you will always have people who follow you. Who listen to you. It is the very way of Human nature. Even when satisfied there are those who wish to have someone to look up to, a person who is smarter, or stronger-to take the burden from their mind when life gets too hard. It all starts with being honest. Not everyone is the full blown Individual, in fact most are not. There is nothing wrong with it, it is a fact of Nature itself and the fact that this Century went blind to, somehow, is one of the baffling mysteries that may never be solved fully. Only ever truly theory, and educated guessing, being the thumbtack that is pushed on the provincial Historical map.

      So let us continue on with the subject of change. Like this Human need to have change go backwards, in an attempt to propel us forward. Now, when this subject is brought up around me, I, like most people, take a bit of a step back mentally until the subject in question is fully expressed. From the fact there use to not be the need for a piece of paper, to verify the amount of knowledge one has, to the fabric of Society and marriage dilemma. It will always be controversial. I want to start with aesthetics, Society would do good for a major shift back to the late 1940s and 1950s appearance wise. In a very weak attempt to eliminate class, weak minded and quite frankly, lazy, Individuals in search of Power: began making looking like someone is broke and miserable the thing to do. This attempt at a classless Society, caused more damage to the mental state of Humanity in the long run, than any attempt ever at creating a classless Society. When people are dressing good, they are feeling good, and as in such feel that they have more than they actually may currently have-materiel wise. This sense of well being is what creates the need to spread the feeling of well being, and thus such, ripples through Society like a rock thrown in still water, until it has made well being the new normal. The lazy attempt I speak of, as us in the first century of the 2000s know, began with the Boomers and their Hippie movement, be free, fuck and love whoever you want, we are all the same, so lets dress the same: we're broke though so dress like us. Now you may be saying "Now Kyle, they worked for that. Came up with ideas for graphic designs etc. They made the money; they can't be lazy." Yes and no. Physicality of work is not the only aspect of work. To love one's neighbor as themselves, and do no harm, throws the concept of work into the mental, inspirational, and spiritual realms. This is one of the first realizations that come to those born into the Socialist Energy. And to demoralize the Human to look more impoverished is an Authoritarian Socialist tactic. Stay down, so I can rise. So to speak. Now that you see, now is always the best time to change, let's continue…

Rationalism and Spiritualism let's get a few things straight.

Now I know what the Atheists are saying, with their rationality on the brink of putting the book down. Hello, lets allow our conversation to begin now. Neither side is going away. Ever. Let me say it again, neither side is going away, ever. Get use to each other. It is the beauty of the first amendment of The United States Constitution. The document recognizes the very fundamental fabric of Human nature and its need to believe in whatever it wants, without fear of persecution, true Freedom of Thought, Feeling, and Speech on all levels. Exactly what Democratic Socialism needs to keep the betterment of the Society at the forefront of conversation. Both sides argue for the same type of security, in oneself and loved ones, just in different ways.

Let me be as blunt as possible, nobody has cared about anybody's beliefs, at all, on any level seriously: since the Boomers came with the Free Love and Peace movement. Being the first of the

American generations to start fully embracing the idea, of us all being equal on a very basic level. But like all generations, who were not at the level of technology, for their lifestyle to fully manifest- they decayed into the greed of the Individual. And its lust for Power. Now youre most likely asking, where does Rationality fit? I see you talking about energies, and overarching themes, and platitudes but no Rationality. The Rationality is in everything I am stating, if all you're looking for is the policy, you're missing the whole reason for the policies development, and the why of its coming about. And to overlook that is not Rational. It is, and always will be, irrational to dismiss anything based off of what someone believes the underlying tone of the Universe is created or controlled by. In fact, it is the same delusional mind state that dismisses the possibility of no Creator, or that the Creator of Humans could be the Anunnaki, the mind in question is just on the side of the isle or belief system: that feels realist to the Individual.

Every Generation is the Greatest Generation, most just get lost in the Individual.

As Napoleon Bonaparte said, "History is a set of lies agreed upon by man.". Think about it like this. A generation that developed the lightbulb, phone, and free electricity if they had chosen to have it, indoor plumbing for those able to afford it. Is it not by far, the Greatest in History for making giant leaps into something more? Revolutionizing the world. But maybe like me, you too already see the flaw, the beginning of the downfall.

Boomers will say, "Well we gave you computers! We gave you intercontinental missiles! We gave you (fill in the blank.)" The Greatest Generation will say "Well we gave everyone indoor plumbing and television. We gave planes and tanks that were Revolutionary to War! We gave (fill in the blank).". What both don't tell you is "We gave you meaningless causes to fight for and expect you to believe they have meaning. We gave you covert, domestic terrorism, in the name of Religions and Economic structures we don't like or understand: to be able to pirate resources from those countries. We gave you the okay, to be wolves in sheep's clothing. We gave you destruction, like those before gave us." Now not all Boomers are like this, there is the Free Love, and Peace movement that swept the nation, the push back if you will, but we all have read or seen how that played out in History. And its reversion into the needs of the Individual. Some of us reading this are still seeing it firsthand.

    Does the title of the essay ring true yet? No? Let us look some more.

    What needs to be looked at is the Historical index of Good, the Generations had done in the world: before any labels have been put in place for who is the Greatest. And, as it has become well known in History, only letting others speak of highly of you brings real honor. Boomers are the ones that named these Generations at first, and then forced their children to call them such. Like every child, ever. Giving more props to the parents than any ancestors before. The so-called Greatest Generation did some Revolutionary things this is true, paper money, moving us off the Tangible Goods standard and on to something more sustaining for the needs of the Individual and their Consumerism. Television and movies. These things for the Consumer in us all, is undeniably great. But they were all built around the workings, teachings, political ideologies, and patented inventions of the previous Generations. Every Generation is the Greatest Generation: most just get lost in the Individual. The Individual says, "If I can see it and I can touch it then its real." Tangibility has ruled the world since the inception of Society. The idea of a money system, backed by only words, was most likely unthinkable. With times being so rough, up to the point of Boomers, as to cause the development of previously mentioned devices.

Millennials pride themselves in being Millennials. The next Transcendental Generation.

Let me explain. We were made to think there are these different Generations when really there are three. Transcendental, Progressive, and Gilded/Golden. The Transcendental change the fabric of Society. Politics, Technology, Ideology, these words represent the impact those born to the Generation have on the world. Progressives, progress what was brought before and make it something better. And of course, those born in the Gilded/Golden Generation reap the benefits. And then the cycle repeats, the Individual's need for something better never ends.

However, we were intentionally stunted. Halted, by the Power and Envy needs of the Individual, spanning both the previous Progressive and Gilded Generations, to remain the Authoritarians in our Socialism. To hold on to a World that no longer existed. One destined for Greater change to come. Most of what the Progressive/Boomer Generation did, is their best to stomp out the Gilded/Generation X, and their understanding of the trying to fulfill the Individual. Enter in the desperate attempt of looking broke. Instead of inspiring Good, they brought a springing of a well of hate and oppression that then was, to be passed down to us, the next Transcendental Generation. Many of whom fell bait line and sinker. Causing the incarnation of self-loathing in the Progressive/Generation Z-Generation. After all the World is so terrible. But like every Gilded Generation, some good did remain coming through, hence inspiring Millennials, like myself to dig deeper into History, to spot the pattern, to continue the Change toward Human thriving not just surviving.

Shaking ourselves Free of the mind state:

"Ignorance of a Matter implies shame, guilt, or lack of Understanding and Intelligence so I must remain: to see the job through."

No longer ignoring the fact that History, only progressed by leaps and bounds, from people who didn't know what they were doing, most of the time.

Mathematics and Physics are prime examples of such leaps and bounds.

Authoritarian Socialism has worn many disguises throughout our History as a Nation. Going as far as changing the names of the Political Parties of the times: to gain the outcomes they are seeking. This is where you say "Kyle. You are trying to change the way we see Politics. Are you not?" I am. To a more honest approach. The party of Freedom and Democracy needs only one party. I am calling for the Authoritarians hidden in the mix to band together as well.

Leave us, you façade of Democratic thinking, call yourselves what you are, the world is ready.

In Society We Trust.

Welcome to Reality. Everyone has their own personal beliefs as to why they can trust living in Society. Trust the Human next to them to not do something crazy. Some say God, others say Reason. Whatever the underlying reason it all boils down to the feeling of security: In Society We Trust. And the Socialisms that are created from it.

Now many would say "Well, I don't trust Society." You live in Society, don't you? You trust it enough to keep risking your life to live in it. "That's not the same, they have made it, so I have to live in Society." No, they didn't. Nothing is stopping you from walking out into the middle of nowhere, building your own little farm and just living there. Catching wild animals to breed as cattle and food, planting your own field of food that grows naturally in your chosen area. You need people, that's why you haven't. It is okay, that's the Nature of Existence. The big question, is there more like me? And better yet, is there a way I don't have to work so hard. Admitting this is the first step in realizing why you need to take more of an interest in the Political structure of Our Socialism. And why Our Socialism needs to be more active in helping its own Individuals thrive, before once again trying to help the rest of the Humans on this planet. Set by example as it were, regaining the light on the hill status. This deep trust for other Conscious beings is one many have come trying to put a wedge in, the reason, to prop up the Greed in the said Individual. As the saying goes, divided we fall. Allowing the Authoritarian Individual to gain more money, Power, and perceived status: causing more Envy within the population in a desperate attempt to fulfill their own selfish needs, and feelings of making History. This leads us into the topic and question of "What can we do about raising our people up? Everyone, so that no singular Individual has Power over the others completely." Is there something we can do? Yes. Will it be easy? Yes. If we choose to make it so. But this is where the fear of change will begin. It takes the revitalizing of the Socialism, so to speak, not a Revolution per say, just a refocusing of priorities. And it starts with not ignoring its obvious title, and calling it all what it is, a Socialism. Having Society speak about this Ism and all its Institutions openly, by name, without fear or judgement. Then comes the major shift of the abilities of the Socialisms influence. What it can and cannot do with the monies it prints. First and foremost, making the Citizenry its true priority. This, having become more important than ever with Automation looming to take over by the 2040s and 50s. So, what do we do? You still haven't answered that you may be saying. So on that note, let's talk about Amendments. Ones we can use continue to the advancement of the Socialism we all belong to and live under. Enter the amendments…

The Consumer Tax Amendment

All taxation, not including the Consumer Tax, is here by revoked. No other taxes can be implemented on the Citizenry without direct voting on a National scale. No Representative of Legislator, Executive, or Judicial office can overturn this amendment. Only a majority vote of seventy five percent of the population, or higher, can overturn it.

A tax of no less than twenty-five percent, and no higher than fifty percent, sales tax, is to be imposed on a National level: of all New and Used items. Starting at twenty-five percent when the amendment is implemented, and is unable to be voted on to raise until ten years after ratification.

The Citizen's and Federal Basic Income Amendment

The Citizen's Basic Income is the Nation's Economical Gross, and its yearly financial income, says is the poverty level of what the Citizenry should be, without the Citizen's Basic Income: Double the poverty level is given yearly, divided in the form of monthly checks.

Those who work for the Federal System, be it Legislative, Judicial, or Executive Branch: receive five times the poverty level of the Nation's Economical Gross of its yearly financial incomes, divided in the form of monthly checks.

No other raising of the Citizen's Basic Income, or the Federal Basic Income is allowed past what is required by the standard of living of the times.

No Federal employee, or elected official, can draw any other form of compensation or monies, while working in or for the United States.

Foreign Policy Amendment

No Treaties requiring an exchange of goods, services, or money can take place unless: The Federal System has funded the Basic Incomes, Education, Housing, Utilities and Yearly Medical expenses of the Citizenry.

No pervious Treaties that were signed before the ratification of this amendment, shall continue to receive any form of aid until: The Federal System has funded the Citizen's Basic Income, The Federal Basic Income, and, the Education, Housing, Utilities and Yearly Medical expenses of the Citizenry.

Retirement Amendment

The age of retirement can not be higher than the age of 60.

No official can be elected, or employed, or stay in any position of the Federal system past, or at, the age of retirement.

The Federal employee, or elected official does not keep the Federal Basic Income pay upon retirement or expulsion from aging out of the Federal system: they revert to only receiving the Citizen's Basic Income.

We are the Millennium. That's why we were called Millennials.

My Generation lived in a time where people saw what was happening, but didn't believe it was happening. The rise of Automation, and the need for this Manifesto, and its revival of the United States of Humanity. The policies on the Individual and its Greed, like Billionaires, or whatever is the highest of "aires" in the future, or what people can and can't do with their bodies, is a matter of debate for the Citizens. And the Socialism of its time. If they still exist when you are reading this. Equality and Freedom of their own incarnation is the ultimate outcome of all Conscious Beings. We as a Species, are a movement of Freethinking Individuals, no longer needing to call Society, and this Socialism, that is a result of our Consciousness, by anything other than the Socialism it truly is. We are not meant to be Governed; we are meant to be Free. Enacting policies that better our Advancement as a Species. Enticing others to join us. To unify. This Nation is to be the ultimate Socialism.

We as the Freedom loving people of this Country, of this Generation, need to band together over our shared needs in these changing times. There is no stopping it, and we must do it by the only way the Individual understands, money. These Amendments and Philosophy of Socialism is a Reality, not an idea. A Reality that Society can get behind but chooses not to, because why? It sounds funny? Like a disorder? How childish for someone claiming to understand Society: to not call something by a name that makes the most sense because you don't like it. Our Socialism doing its job, while also actively ensuring the Citizen's needs, this is what will save the rise of the Human Species. Not what the Authoritarians think we need. Trying its best to take away the Individual's decisions. Drugs, Alcohol, and Guns just to name a few but the list can go on. Don't be blinded by the Fear of Change, stay strong and spread the Truth. As the Wise men say, "Be the Change you wish to see in the World."

Be the Change in your Socialism, that's what you were meant to be Millennial/Transcendental Generation. The fight with the Authoritarian doesn't end until it is forced out of the Atmosphere of the planet you are on. Your World is ready, they are just waiting on you.

I could go on with other policies and speak on them more. Like my stance on billionaires and my firm belief that: A billionaire is not a Capitalist. A billionaire is an Individual trying to be an Authoritarian on Society using money, in most cases: stationing themselves in positions that put them above the established Socialism. That is a domestic terrorist to the Socialism. One doing its best to overthrow our collective, Democratic Authority. Or my stance on complete freedom of speech, thought, expression, and religion as a Good on society. To my agreement of gun ownership of everyone, regardless of criminal status. If everyone is carrying, and trained, to the point of having training in high school: in preparation for the Authoritarians at large of their time-will most likely be a necessity until the numbers of the Power obsessed Individuals dwindle into Space. And then all weapons can be focused into making sure no hostiles come back toward the Socialism.

But these are my Beliefs that's the beauty of Democratic Socialism, of us who love Freedom, who want to help the Human thrive and not just survive. We can debate what we think the solution is and let the Citizen's decide. These Amendments are the jolt the Socialism needs, before its too late. Before Automation crashes the Human worker and the economy anyway. For those of you reading in my lifetime. For those of you in the future, I can only hope the world has seen the Light. Hopefully this Manifesto helped you to better understand the struggle of the first century, as we progressed to where you are now.

What you hold in your hand is the answer, I can only pray those of you in the future are enjoying the benefits of these Amendments and Philosophy. The Authoritarian can't win. We must not let it, stand together, make the monopoly board fair for all Citizens and Federal employees.

Be they Military, Legislative or Executive. It is time to stop pretending we are not equal, and just be equal. Let those who want to save the money and build better lives, save the money, and build better lives. And those who just want to live, let them just live. It won't stop the Individual in Humans from wanting more. Just like Automation will take over soon, and already has taken over, for our time travelers, like all Greed, it will leave eventually: off to find something more in the Universe. It is not some foreign concept, it's the goal of this entire energy, of this Socialism within us all. To live in peace and harmony with each other, going through existence feeling safe, feeling at Home. So, I ask you: Do you have what it takes to be a bringer of Democratic-Socialism of your time? I guess History will tell.

    To all my fellow Socialist reading this before my Death, I'll see you in the struggle. Just a reminder: Authoritarians fall, Democracy swallows them whole.

New and Used Grammar for a New Perception.

This is a blueprint to help those who wish to know how to address those working in Socialism.

The Executive Branch of Socialism:

I am a (insert policy style here) Socialist I oversee the Executive Branch of the Socialism Institution, or President.

Legislative Branch of Socialism:

I am a Legislative Socialist, or Legislator.

Judicial Branch of Socialism:

I am a Judicial Socialist, or Judge.

Addressing the Military: I am a Military Socialist; I work in the Army division. (Navy, Air Force, and Space Force)

All other Socialism employees:

I am a Socialist. I work for the Socialism building doing (insert job description here, this includes construction workers).

Citizen: I am a Citizen of the United States of America, and the Socialism it has created.

All Socialism buildings are called as such, when addressing the Nation at large:

"The Legislative Branch of Socialism enacted policies today…" replacing Legislative with Judicial or Executive when necessary.

The Declaration of Democratic Socialism and its Socialists

In the course of Human History there comes a point where all ideas must be revisited. This revisiting must be for the purpose of keeping the Nation and the Individual strong, the people thriving, not just surviving. For the Individual in us all to try and fulfill the need to change something, anything, for the better. It is also common in Nature to find the Individual squabbling over what is perceived as theirs in their youth: sometimes well into maturity. But eventually changing and growing in time, realizing the need and security, which can only be fulfilled with Society and with the other Individuals. Some will claim it is God, others will try to explain it away with Reason. No matter what it is being called by in Society it is none the less an ism within the Fabric of Consciousness. From this Force of Nature comes the Creation of shared

Ideals, written down and upheld by one another. Ideals on the ways to stop the dark of the Individual and from its ability to kill, maim, or destroy any facet of the peaceful life trying to be established. This, coming together, this Democratic consensus- has many ways of going about finding solutions. They debate on the proper ways to do it, but ultimately find common ground, every time. Because to not so, invites the Authoritarian to step in and "fix" the issue. Whether or not, the idea is even worth its weight in merit. As a Freedom loving Individual, one who wishes only to be a force of Good, I stand against that Power. I stand with Democracy and Consciousness coming together to solve whatever may arise. I stand for the Democratic-Socialism of The United States and its Territories.

I AM A DEMOCRATIC SOCIALIST.

Made in the USA
Columbia, SC
09 June 2024